DATE DUE			

C2

GUMDROP BOOKS - Bethany, Missouri

AKAMBA

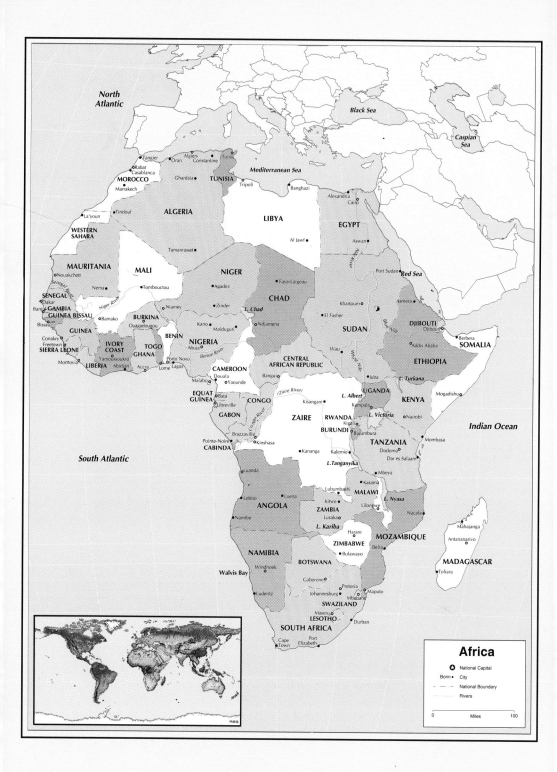

North
Atlantic

Black Sea

Caspian
Sea

Tangier
Oran Algiers Constantine Tunis
Rabat
Casablanca
MOROCCO   Ghardaia   TUNISIA   Tripoli
Marrakech   Banghazi
Mediterranean Sea
Alexandria
Cairo

La'youn   Tindouf
ALGERIA   LIBYA   EGYPT
WESTERN
SAHARA   Tamanrasset   Al Jawf   Aswan

MAURITANIA   MALI   NIGER   Port Sudan   Red Sea
Nouakchott
Nema   Tombouctou   Agadez   Faya-Largeau   Asmera
SENEGAL   Khartoum
Dakar   Niamey   Zinder   CHAD   DJIBOUTI
Banjul GAMBIA   L. Chad   El Fasher   Djibouti
GUINEA BISSAU   Bamako   BURKINA   Ndjamena   Berbera
Bissau   Ouagadougou   Kano   SUDAN   SOMALIA
GUINEA   Maiduguri   Addis Ababa
Conakry   BENIN   NIGERIA   Wau   ETHIOPIA
Freetown   IVORY   Abuja   White Nile   Juba   L. Turkana
SIERRA LEONE COAST TOGO   Benue River   CENTRAL   UGANDA
Monrovia   Yamoussoukro GHANA Porto Novo   AFRICAN REPUBLIC   Mogadishu
LIBERIA   Abidjan Accra Lome Lagos   CAMEROON   Bangui   L. Albert   KENYA
Douala   Kisangani   Kampala
EQUAT. Bata Yaounde   (Zaire River)   L. Victoria   Nairobi
GUINEA Libreville CONGO   RWANDA   L. Victoria
Malabo   ZAIRE   Kigali
GABON   BURUNDI Bujumbura   Indian Ocean
Pointe-Noire Brazzaville   Kalemie   TANZANIA   Mombasa
CABINDA Kinshasa   Kananga   Dodoma
Kanaga   Dar es Salaam
South Atlantic   Kalemie
L.Tanganyika
Mbeya
Kasama
Luanda   Lubumbashi   MALAWI   L. Nyasa
Lobito Luena   Kitwe   Lilongwe   Nacala
ANGOLA   ZAMBIA
Namibe   Lusaka   L. Kariba
Harare   MOZAMBIQUE
ZIMBABWE   Beira
NAMIBIA   BOTSWANA   Bulawayo   Mahajanga
Windhoek   Antananarivo
Walvis Bay   Gaborone
Luderitz   Johannesburg Pretoria Maputo MADAGASCAR
Mbabane   Toliara
SWAZILAND
Maseru
Cape Port LESOTHO Durban
Town Elizabeth
SOUTH AFRICA

Africa

⊛ National Capital
Bonn • City
- - - National Boundary
—— Rivers

0   Miles   100

The Heritage Library of African Peoples

AKAMBA

Tiyambe Zeleza, Ph.D.

THE ROSEN PUBLISHING GROUP, INC.
NEW YORK

Published in 1995 by The Rosen Publishing Group, Inc.
29 East 21st Street, New York, NY 10010

First Edition

Manufactured in the United States of America

Library of Congress Cataloging-in-Publication Data

Zeleza, Tiyambe.
    Akamba / Tiyambe Zeleza.
      p. cm. — (The Heritage library of African peoples)
    Includes bibliographical references and index.
    ISBN 0-8239-1768-1
    1. Akamba (African people)—History—Juvenile literature.
  2. Akamba (African people)—Social life and customs—Juvenile literature. [1. Akamba (African people)] I. Title. II. Series.
DT433.545.K36Z45   1994
960'.049639—dc20   94-13614
                                        CIP
                                        AC

Contents

INTRODUCTION

THERE IS EVERY REASON FOR US TO KNOW something about Africa and to understand its past and the way of life of its peoples. Africa is a rich continent that has for centuries provided the world with art, culture, labor, wealth, and natural resources. It has vast mineral deposits, fossil fuels, and commercial crops.

But perhaps most important to us is the fact that fossil evidence indicates that human beings originated in Africa. The earliest traces of human beings and their tools are almost two million years old. Their descendants have migrated throughout the world. To be human is to be of African descent.

The experiences of the peoples who stayed in Africa are as rich and as diverse as of those who left to establish themselves elsewhere. This series of books describe their environment, their modes of subsistence, their relationships, and their customs and beliefs that are to be found on the African continent. They demonstrate the historical linkages between African peoples and the way contemporary Africa has been affected by European colonial rule.

Africa is large, complex, and diverse. It encompasses an area of more than 11,700,000

square miles. The United States, Europe, and India could fit easily into it. The sheer size is an indication of its great variety in geography, terrain, climate, flora, fauna, peoples, languages, and cultures.

Much of contemporary Africa has been shaped by European colonial rule, industrialization, urbanization, and the demands of a world economic system. For more than seventy years, large regions of Africa were ruled by Great Britain, France, Belgium, Portugal, and Spain. African peoples from various ethnic, linguistic, and cultural backgrounds were brought together to form colonial states.

For decades Africans struggled to gain their independence. It was not until after World War II that the colonial territories became independent African states. Today, almost all of Africa is ruled by Africans. Large numbers of Africans live in modern cities. Rural Africa is also being transformed, and yet its peoples still engage in many of their age-old customs and beliefs.

Contemporary circumstances and natural events have not always been kind to ordinary Africans. Today, however, new popular social movements and technological innovations pose great promise for Africa's future development.

George C. Bond
Institute of African Studies
Columbia University, New York City

By the sixteenth century, the Akamba were settled around Mt. Kilimanjaro.

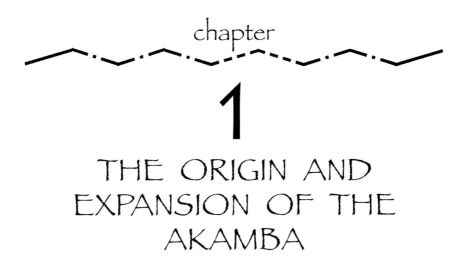

THE ORIGIN AND EXPANSION OF THE AKAMBA

ACCORDING TO MOST AKAMBA ORAL traditions, by the beginning of the sixteenth century ancestors of the Akamba were settled around Mount Kilimanjaro in present-day Kenya. Only one section, the Mumoni group, believes it originated on the coast. It is not clear exactly when the Akamba first came to the Kilimanjaro region, but they began leaving the plains in the late sixteenth century.

They migrated for several reasons. Often raided for their cattle by the Maasai, the Akamba sought greater security. In addition, the region was becoming overpopulated. Consequently, the Akamba needed an area that was more productive for farming, livestock-keeping, and hunting.

The Akamba settled around the Chyulu hills, and later on the Kibwezi plains, but there

SUDAN

Lokitaung

•Lokiehokio

Lake
Turkana

ETHIOPIA

Lodwar•

•Buna

Turkwel R.

Lokichar•

Marsabit Mts.

Marsabit•

UGANDA

Ndoto Mts.

Milgis River

Wajir•

Kerio R.

Maralal

Mado Gashi •

•Kitale

Uaso Nyiro River

SOMALIA

•Eldoret

Lake Baringo

Liboi

Mt. Kenya

Kisumu•

Nakuru•

Nyeri•

Embu•

AKAMBA

•Garissa

•Kericho

Lake Victoria

Tana River

Thika•

Kitui
District

Nairobi

Thika•

Athi R.

Machakos
District

Lamu•

Chyulu hills

Athi R.

TANZANIA

Kibwezi
Plains

Mt. Kilimanjaro

Galana River

Malindi•

Voi•

Mombasa•

Indian
Ocean

AFRICA (KENYA)

KENYA

⩶ Mountains
------- International Boundaries

they encountered long droughts. In the mid-seventeenth century the Akamba migrants turned toward the Mbooni hills. Here they found a region that was fertile and well watered, with dense forests and many buffalo.

Even today the Akamba practice many of the rituals and ceremonies important to their ancestors.

As Akamba settlements grew, the forest gradually gave way to fields, grazing areas, and villages. The population increased considerably, as did the livestock herds. As grazing land became scarce, some people moved to the plains

11

The land that the Akamba inhabit is called the Ukambani.

of central Kitui across the Athi River. In later years others migrated from the Mbooni hills in search of farming land.

These migrations into the present-day Kamba districts of Kitui and Machakos were not of large groups. Individual families or small groups of kinsmen gradually filtered out, in search of more fertile lands and prospects for a better life.

These migrations changed the Akamba into a

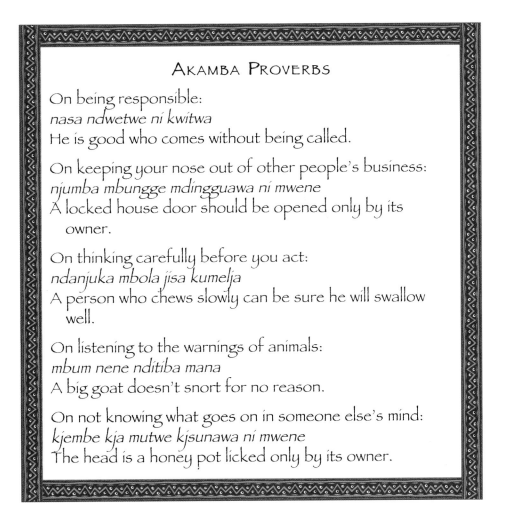

AKAMBA PROVERBS

On being responsible:
nasa ndwetwe ni kwitwa
He is good who comes without being called.

On keeping your nose out of other people's business:
njumba mbungge mdingguawa ni mwene
A locked house door should be opened only by its
  owner.

On thinking carefully before you act:
ndanjuka mbola jisa kumelja
A person who chews slowly can be sure he will swallow
  well.

On listening to the warnings of animals:
mbum nene nditiba mana
A big goat doesn't snort for no reason.

On not knowing what goes on in someone else's mind:
kjembe kja mutwe kjsunawa ni mwene
The head is a honey pot licked only by its owner.

mixed community. They came to occupy regions
with varied ecological conditions, which gave
rise to different economic activities. Separate
dialects emerged in Machakos and Kitui as
groups intermingled with other communities.

The Akamba communities were similar to
most of their neighbors, especially the Agikuyu,
the Embu, and the Meru. The people depended

on farming and livestock-rearing. They lived in small settlements organized along family lines. Their social and cultural institutions had many many similarities. In fact, the languages were closely related, belonging to the Bantu group.

Among the sprawling Akamba, Kikuyu, Embu, and Meru-speaking settlements, people thought of themselves as members of societies rather than ethnic groups. The agricultural peoples of Central Kenya, including the Akamba, drew a sharp distinction between themselves and the pastoral Maasai. Their strongest associations centered on family, lineage, and locality.

Localities were dependent on one another in the region. They varied widely in rainfall, good soil, and wealth. Local and regional trading networks began to develop. The regional system was primarily based on the exchange of food and livestock products. The Kamba-speaking peoples played a major role in its development.▲

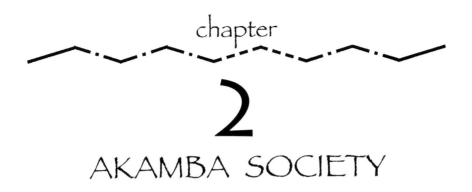

chapter

2
AKAMBA SOCIETY

THE FAMILY WAS THE BASIC AKAMBA SOCIAL unit. Several families that could trace their descent to a common ancestor were called *mbai*, often translated as clan. Descent was through the father's line, but land and other property were inherited by sons from their mother. A husband usually gave his wife land that she would work. Her sons received the land after her death.

The membership of clans varied greatly. A large clan had as many as several thousand people. There were clans of blacksmiths, honey hunters, rainmakers, and healers. Clans held their members together and protected their interests.

Marriage was not allowed between members of the same clan. Each clan had its own cattle brand, arrowhead mark, and totem, usually an

animal. Characteristics of the totem animal were thought to be shared by members of the clan. A person was not allowed to kill or eat one of his totem animals or touch it if he found it dead.

▼ AGE GRADES ▼

In addition to the clan system, age grades were a major feature of Akamba social organization. A person entered a new age grade every time he reached an important life change.

A male Akamba went through seven stages. Up to the age of two and before weaning, he was known as *kakenge*. Between two and six he was called *kaana*. An uncircumcised boy from seven to thirteen was a *kavisi*. He usually herded cattle and began to learn other social roles. Circumcision was performed before the boy completed puberty at fifteen or sixteen.

Akamba males went through three initiation ceremonies. The first, *nzaiko ila nini*, could be carried out at the age of five or six. The second, *nzaiko ila nene*, was conducted at puberty. The third was a secret ceremony reserved for selected men over the age of forty.

From the ages of seventeen to twenty-seven, a man entered the age group *anake*, sometimes translated as warriors. The *anake* were allowed to marry and have children. They were not permitted to drink beer because, as the protectors of the community, they were supposed to be

alert at all times. This prohibition was removed when the *anake* reached the next age grade, the *nthele*.

Men in the *nthele* group ranged from twenty-nine to forty years of age. To be accepted, a man had to pay a fee of one to three goats. To enter the elders, or *atumia*, men of fifty and older, the fee was either one steer or ten goats.

The elders were divided into three groups. The lowest rank, the *atumia ma kisuka*, were the county elders. They were responsible for counseling about peace and war, burials, and communal work like digging watering holes in times of drought.

The top groups were the *atumia ma ithembo*, or religious elders, and the *atumia ma nzama*, elders of the council. These groups served as judges, counselors, and ritual and religious leaders.

Females were also divided into age groups. Like the boys, they were called *kaana* up to the age of seven. Between eight and eleven they were *kelitu*, and at the age of twelve they became *mwiitu*. Girls went through two initiation ceremonies, after which they were called *aka*. Finally there were the elderly women, the *kiveti*. Like their male counterparts, the *kiveti* were divided into groups, the *kiveti sya ithembo* and the *kiveti sya nzama*. These women took part in some rituals conducted by the male elders.

Male elders are divided into three groups, female elders into two groups.

▼ MARRIAGE ▼

A marriage was not simply an alliance between a couple but also between their families. When a young man met a woman he liked, his father would approach the young woman's father. If both men agreed to the marriage, the young man's mother visited the young woman's mother to make sure that she too was satisfied.

To formalize the relationship, the suitor sent goats to the woman's family. Further gifts of beer and goats followed, leading up to negotiations as to the number of livestock the young man would pay as *bridewealth*. The payment of bridewealth is often spread over many years.

Akamba men could have more than one wife. This practice is called polygamy. To marry another woman, a man had to get the permission of his father as well as his wife. A man could also inherit his brother's widow as a wife if the woman agreed.

Divorce was rare. The families of the couple concerned would try to patch up disputes. The parents or guardians, assisted by other elders, acted as marriage counselors. If necessary, they would suggest a separation rather than outright divorce.

A man could divorce his wife for laziness, unfaithfulness, or practicing witchcraft. A woman could divorce her husband on grounds of cruelty.

Girls between the ages of eight and eleven are in an age group called the *kelitu*.

Divorce called for the return of the bride-wealth. The divorced woman could return to her husband at any time before the bridewealth had been returned. The return of bridewealth could be done in stages. Usually it was done after the woman had remarried.

▼ POLITICAL STRUCTURE ▼

The smallest unit of territory in Akamba society was the *musyi* or homestead. It could house a single extended family or several families. Authority within the homestead lay with the family head, or in the male elders if the homestead had several families. The elders met in the men's outdoor fireplace, called *thome*, to discuss issues and make decisions.

Several homesteads made up a village or *utui*. A village could contain several clans. Each village had its own council of elders, judges, and war leaders.

Several villages made up a *kivalo*, or district, the largest territorial grouping. Each *kivalo* had a common ground where ceremonies and age-grade transitions took place.

Disputes involving villages were brought to the elders of the *kivalo*. The basic principle of Akamba law was compensation rather than punishment, whether the case was murder, theft, or unpaid debts.

In times of war, warriors were recruited from

Both of an Akamba woman's parents must approve of a man before he can marry their daugher.

the entire *kivalo*. The army was divided into four squads: scouts or spies; a squad to seize war booty, especially cattle; the main fighting squad; and a reserve squad.

22

This is an example of a typical Akamba hut.

Despite sharing the same culture, the Akamba, like their Central Kenyan neighbors, did not belong to a unified political entity. Power in independent districts and villages rested in the hands of elders rather than with all-powerful chiefs or kings, as was the case in many other parts of Africa.▲

chapter

3

FARMING AND TRADE

The Akamba depended on a mixed economy of farming and cattle-herding. They preferred to plant their fields along the banks of rivers and on the slopes in the highland areas. The highlands received more rain than the low-lying areas. In the river valleys they irrigated their fields with ditches. On the slopes they cut terraces to keep the soil from eroding.

▼ INTERCROPPING ▼

The main crops were grains such as sorghum, maize, and millet. Also grown were peas, beans, sweet potatoes, yams, cassava, bananas, and sugarcane. Several crops were usually grown on the same field. This system of cultivation, called intercropping, was widely practiced by farmers throughout Africa.

Intercropping had several advantages. It re-

The Akamba built huts in the millet fields to scare birds away from the crops.

duced erosion because the combination of crops provided soil cover from harmful sun rays and reduced the growth of weeds. Different plants growing together were less likely to be attacked by the same pests. In addition, the risk of drought was lessened, because different crops required different amounts of water.

When necessary, especially when land was being cleared or during weeding and harvesting,

Everyone takes a part in preparing the grain for consumption—this man is husking millet.

workparties of neighbors, called *mwethya*, were organized.

▼ LAND OWNERSHIP ▼

Land was held jointly by an extended family, although individuals could work their own plots. Men were the primary landowners, and they could obtain land by inheritance or purchase. An owner who had bought land could do as he liked with it. But when he died the land became the property of his family.

Land was also farmed by tenants, who usually paid the owner of the land with a portion of his produce or with labor. If the owner was dissatisfied, the tenant could be evicted. If all went well, the tenant's children could inherit the tenancy rights.

▼ LIVESTOCK ▼

Ukambani, as the land occupied by the Akamba is called, lacked a regular water supply. Because of this, the Akamba learned not to rely on crop cultivation. Livestock were an important feature of the economy.

Cattle were the most highly valued animals. Like the Maasai and other peoples of the region, the Akamba mostly kept the short-horned zebu. The herds were often split up and sent to graze in widely separated villages. In some parts of Ukambani, livestock were moved to different

regions depending on the season. This practice is called *transhumance.*

A family or an individual could gain grazing rights to pastureland by building and occupying a cattle post. Such land was called *kisese.* The land returned to common ownership if it was not regularly used.

Livestock provided the Akamba with meat, milk, and butter. The animal skins were used to make clothing, hats, bags, and sandals. Owning a large herd was a sign of wealth.

▼ HUNTING AND CRAFTSMANSHIP ▼

The Akamba were renowned hunters, famous for their poisoned arrows. They were good at trapping, too. Each family also kept a beehive. Honey was an important part of the diet.

The Akamba manufactured a wide range of crafts. Some specialists made iron tools, weapons, and ornaments. Iron production required the skills of mining, smelting, and smithing. Others made wooden implements, including furniture, boxes, musical instruments, and utensils. The arts of pottery, basketry, and leatherwork were quite highly developed.

▼ TRADING ▼

The Akamba were probably the greatest traders of nineteenth-century Kenya. Some say they developed long-distance trade because

Ukambani was so prone to drought and famine. Others attribute their trading success to the fact that they were good hunters. From elephants they obtained large quantities of ivory, which was in great demand at the coast. The Akamba were also used to migration, which made it easy for them to travel long distances.

There were three kinds of trading activity among the Akamba: local trade with other Akamba, regional trade, and long-distance trade.

Ukambani had great differences in climate and soils, family size, and resources. Consequently, the Akamba localities and families regularly traded with each other.

Trade took place between the Akamba and their neighbors, including the Kikuyu, Embu, Meru, and Maasai. The Akamba sold ivory products, tobacco, clothes, iron implements, ritual objects, and poisons to the Kikuyu and bought from them food staples, pottery and basketry, herbal medicines, spears, and cattle.

The Akamba were the leading long-distance traders. Trading caravans took ivory to the coast of Kenya and sold it to the Swahili and Arab traders for textiles, metal, and jewelry.

Trading associations were formed to conduct interregional and long-distance trade. Five to twenty Akamba would pool their resources to organize a caravan. They planned strategies, routes, and destinations and traveled as a group.

Two examples of intricate Akamba sculpture.

Usually they took an oath of allegiance to one another.

Goods in the long-distance trade were transported by porters on foot. Many of the porters were recruited from the poorer strata of society. Some joined for the adventure of travel or to acquire skills and capital to establish their own trading enterprises. They were paid in goods.

The Akamba are noted for their craftsmanship in woodcarving.

AKAMBA MUSICAL INSTRUMENTS

The Akamba play many kinds of musical instruments. They have wind, string, and percussion instruments, just as in Western music, and each makes it own special sound. But unlike the instruments you would see in a rock band or symphony orchestra, Akamba instruments are often made out of plants and sometimes only last a few days.

The *ndumali* is like an oboe. It is a wind instrument with a reed, so it has a very nasal sound. The *ndumali* is made of a giant grass called *mbilu*. It has a corn husk for a bell at the end, to make it a little louder.

Other wind instruments are the *mukata* and *mutulitu*, with a more mellow sound than the *ndumali*. The *mukata* is made of two pieces of bamboo. The player looks to be blowing into two recorders at once. The *mutulitu* is played like a flute.

Several stringed instruments are made of gourds or even tin containers and strung with animal tendons. The *uta na nzele* is plucked like a banjo, whereas the *mbeve* is bowed like a violin.

As with most African peoples, drums are the most important musical instruments of the Akamba. They have many varieties, each of which is used for a particular ceremony or dance. The main types of drum are the *kyaa, ngoma, ngutha, mbalya,* and *kithemba.*

Conducting long-distance trade was a profitable but difficult enterprise. As a security measure, traders established a relationship called *giciaro* with another traveler on the route. The two became "blood brothers," a kinship that linked not only them but their families.

The Akamba began to lose their dominance over long-distance trade in the 1840s. The

The Akamba sold many products to their neighbors, including ebony carvings.

elephant herds had dwindled in many parts of Ukambani. At the same time, the coastal Swahili and Arab traders began coming into the interior of the continent. By the 1860s they were trading regularly as far west as Uganda. Many Akamba traders were reduced to the role of agents or middlemen for the coastal traders.

The impact of interregional and long-distance trade on the Akamba and other peoples of Central Kenya was significant and varied. Through it new crops such as maize and cassava were introduced. It also boosted regional production. The Swahili language and the Islamic

religion spread into the interior from the coast. At the same time, Akamba traders remained at the coast, establishing permanent communities.

The trade had a negative impact as well, however. The large-scale importation of guns for elephant hunting made warfare more deadly. In addition to ivory, the Akamba appear to have entered the coastal slave trade and to have kept slaves at home. The growth of both the slave trade and local slavery undermined the communities involved. Moreover, many of the powerful traders became political rulers who cared more for personal profit than the well-being of their society.

▼ DIVISION OF LABOR ▼

As in other societies of Central Kenya, responsibilities were divided according to gender and age among the Akamba. The men's tasks included tending livestock, clearing fields, building roads, bridges, houses, and granaries, hunting and fighting, making utensils, tanning leather and making clothes, and collecting honey. Men planted specific crops, such as bananas, yams, sweet potatoes, sugarcane, and tobacco. They also had various legal and ritual duties.

In addition to child care, women were responsible for thatching and plastering houses, making pottery and baskets, sewing, storing food, cooking, fetching water and firewood,

Long-distance trade involved crossing rivers and traversing difficult terrain. Mt. Kilimanjaro is shown in the background here.

grinding grain and pounding sugarcane for beer, milking cows, and churning butter. In cultivation, women planted corn, millet, and beans and did the hoeing, weeding, and harvesting. Women also had certain ritual duties depending on the status of their husbands.

Both men and women participated in iron production; the women collected the ore, and the men smelted it. Trade in livestock was generally monopolized by men, while women controlled trading in grain. Women were most active in local and interregional trade. Their involvement in long-distance trade appears to have been limited.

THE LION, THE HYENA, AND THEIR CATTLE

This is a trickster tale, a story of a clever animal that out-smarts the strength of another animal.

Once upon a time the lion and the hyena went on a cattle raid. The lion stole seven male cattle, and the hyena took seven females. They led their herds back to the village and looked after them for many nights. One morning the lion noticed that one of the hyena's cows had given birth during the night. The lion took some blood and spread it on one of his bulls. Then he stole the newborn calf and put it near the bull.

When the hyena awoke, the lion said, "One of my bulls has given birth to a calf!" The hyena snorted, "Ha! Bulls can't have babies." "But look," argued the lion, "my bull is covered with blood from the birth." Well, the hyena didn't want to argue with the fierce lion, so she suggested that they ask the elders to act as judges.

The next morning the elders came to have a look. They all secretly agreed that the bull could not possibly have borne a calf. However, they were afraid of making the lion angry, so they announced, "The lion's bull has had a calf." The hyena was furious but refused to give up.

As the hyena went in search of other elders to ask for help, she came upon the hare. "Would you come and help me with a lawsuit?" she asked. The hare liked to show off what a clever fellow he was, so he agreed to come the next morning.

Sure enough, when the second group of elders had gathered to judge the case, the hare showed up, carrying gourds. "Hey, where are you going?" asked the lion. The hare answered, "I need to fetch water to wash my father, because he just gave birth to a child." "What?" cried the lion. "A man can't have a baby!"

"Oh, ho! I've caught you," replied the hare. "Didn't you just say that your bull gave birth to a calf?" The hare hopped away before the lion could pounce on him. And the elders all agreed with the proof and gave the calf back to its rightful owner.

Akamba women have many responsibilities, including thatching and plastering houses and taking care of the children.

Wealthy families could afford to hire extra help for the many tasks required to run a household.

Many tasks were performed by children. The job of tending cattle fell largely to boys. Girls did household chores, especially fetching water and firewood and grinding grain. In a family without sons, girls took over the task of grazing the animals.

Rich families, especially those involved in long-distance trade, could hire extra help. Dependent labor could also be obtained. Young boys worked as indentured servants or apprentices. Young women also served as dependent labor during periods of food shortage.▲

chapter

4

RELIGIOUS BELIEFS

THE AKAMBA BELIEVE IN THE EXISTENCE OF God, whom they call Mulungu, the Creator and Preserver of all things. They also call him Mumbi or Mwatuangwi. Mulungu created and brought the first man and woman out of a hole in the ground or, according to another myth, from the sky. The couple were left to bear children and keep the human species going. They brought with them cattle, sheep, and goats.

According to Akamba legend, people were created to live forever. But the chameleon, whom Mulungu had sent to tell them this news, lingered along the way and stammered in delivering the message. Mulungu then sent the fast-flying weaverbird with a message that people were to die. The weaverbird delivered that message before the chameleon had finished telling them of their immortality. That is when people began to die.

Purifying Rituals

If there is sickness in a village and many people are suffering and dying, the head elder may ask a medicine man to perform rituals to purify the village.

In one ritual, special plants are used to make medicine. Two small children are chosen to lead a goat in a circle around all the villagers. The ear of the goat is cut and its blood dripped into a gourd and mixed with the medicine. Then all the people run to the west, toward the sunset, and must not look back. The medicine man throws the herbs and blood on the ground, after which the people may return to their purified village.

The Akamba believe that disasters are sometimes caused by the spirit (*limu*) of an ancestor who is offended at something. Then it is necessary to make a gift to the spirit. Sometimes a fowl is sacrificed to feed the *limu*. The medicine man may have the women make porridge; the sick person and his friends each eat a spoonful then throw a spoonful on the floor to feed the angry spirit. They make the same sort of sacrifice with beer and meat.

When crops fail, it is almost as frightening as illness. Special rituals are held to purify fields. A farmer may bury a bird's egg in a hole in his field to ward off evil. Then he plants over it a branch of *kindio*, a very strong tree. So he prays to Mulungu to keep his crops as strong as the branch.

The Akamba believe Mulungu is all-powerful and all-knowing. He is also merciful and kind. He provides people with life, fertility, rain, and health and protects them from danger, illness, and anxiety. To the Akamba, rain, which they think of as Mulungu's saliva, is his greatest gift to humans.

Mulungu is recognized as a single powerful being, but other divinities and spiritual beings represent his different activities.

The spirits of the departed, the *aimu*, are divided into those who have died up to three or four generations ago and those who died many generations back. To the Akamba, death does not mean an end. The spirits merely go to the spirit world. Death destroys only the body.

To the Akamba, the *aimu* are controlled by Mulungu, who sometimes uses them as messengers. Some of the *aimu* are friendly and benevolent, others are malevolent. Most, however, are both good and evil, like human beings. Possession by spirits is not unusual, especially during important ceremonies and rituals.

Worship among the Akamba involves sacrifices and offerings. Sacrifices, often of an animal, to God or the spirits are made on great occasions, such as rites of passage, planting and harvest, epidemic, war, and drought. Offerings consist of foods, beverages, or other items. Families frequently make offerings to their ancestral spirits.▲

chapter

5

BRITISH COLONIAL RULE

IN 1889 REPRESENTATIVES OF THE IMPERIAL British East African Company (IBEA) set up a trading station in the town of Machakos in central Kenya. From this time on, life among the Akamba changed drastically. Europeans, particularly Germans and British, looking to increase their trade routes, had begun to colonize East Africa. By force, the British took control of Kenya, and the Akamba, like many other African peoples, began to lose their independence.

The intitial goal of the IBEA was to control the long-distance trade of Ukambani.

The Akamba, already distrustful of the newcomers, suffered many criminal acts at the hands of the colonists: theft, rape, and destruction of property and religious shrines. Many Akamba organized boycotts and raids on the

trading stations. Others, however, made alliances with the newcomers in order to obtain guns and new trade goods. The era of the IBEA ended in 1895 when the British government established the East African Protectorate, as Kenya became known.

The British government was not interested merely in trade, but in political control. This was resisted by many Akamba, who fought several battles against the colonial forces. Their resistance was weakened, however, by a series of natural disasters and the great famine of 1897–1901 that devastated central Kenya.

Droughts, locust invasions, and an infectious cattle disease called rinderpest destroyed land and animals. Epidemics of smallpox and influenza, diseases to which the Akamba had no immunity, decimated the population.

Families tried various strategies to survive. Some turned to trade. The poor sold their labor. Some men sent junior wives back to their families. Parents pawned children to wealthier families. Entire families migrated.

By 1901 families and groups that had broken up or migrated returned and began rebuilding their lives. But their world was no longer the same. In the meantime, the British colonial government had strengthened its control over Ukambani and all Kenya.

In little more than a decade the Akamba had

been transformed from an independent people into colonial subjects.

▼ COLONIAL GOVERNMENT ▼

Once in power, the British had to decide how best to govern Kenya. They understood the importance of using local chiefs as part of the administrative system. The problem was that the Akamba did not have chiefs. So the British invented them. In 1902 a law was passed calling for village headmen to enforce colonial orders. A headman was appointed for each *kivalo*. The *kivalo* were grouped into larger territories called locations and placed under these chiefs.

Few of the headmen or chiefs were named from among the elders. Most of them supported the colonial authorities. Becoming a chief was a means of gaining wealth and power.

The councils of elders gradually lost their power to the colonial chiefs. Many Akamba opposed the chiefs and the corruption they represented. Around 1910, the government took away some of the powers of the chiefs.

Attempts were made to restore the councils of elders and make them work side by side with the chiefs. But the system did not work smoothly. The elders were reluctant to arrest tax delinquents, and they did not want to force young men to work outside of Ukambani. In addition, Akamba and British ideas of justice were in

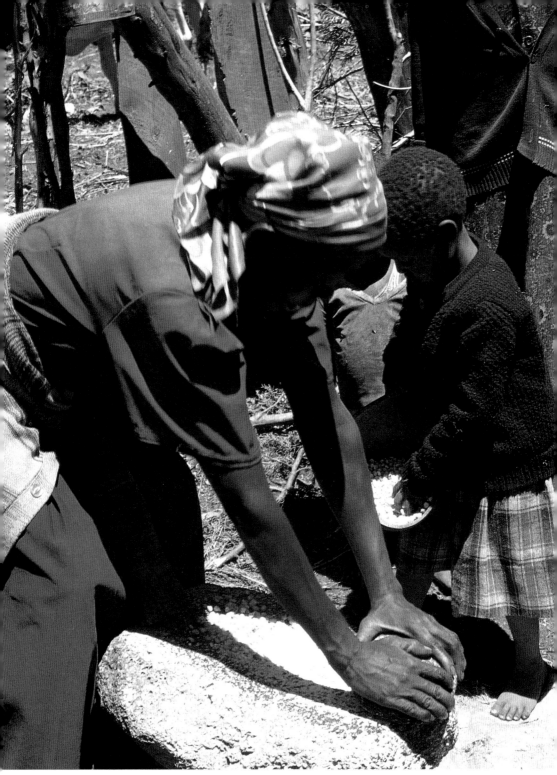

The Akamba believed that schoolwork interfered with their children's chores.

basic conflict. Under the Akamba system, wrongdoers paid compensation to their victims. The British legal system generally demanded punishment.

▼ COLONIAL EDUCATION ▼

In the 1920s a few educated Akamba began to gain power and prestige beyond those of the councils of elders. By the 1930s the basis of power in Akamba society had shifted. Members of the new elite were relatively young, and many had come from poor backgrounds.

The educated elite were largely taught in mission schools. The first Christian mission in Ukambani was established in 1895. But at first, they had difficulty attracting children.

The Akamba did not find Christianity very different from their own religion, but it made little sense to them to abandon their beliefs. In addition, they did not always trust the missionaries.

Parents saw little practical value in mission education. Schoolwork interfered with the children's farm and family chores. To attract pupils, the missionaries even offered to pay the children to come to school. That scheme was abandoned after students went on strike in 1905, demanding more money.

The first Akamba attracted to the mission stations and schools were the poor and outcasts

of society. Many were young, orphaned or abandoned during the famine of the 1890s. Some were girls who had run away from home.

The schools began to gain popularity during the 1920s. By then, colonial rule appeared permanent. It was clear that the people with education had the best jobs and the most money.

The Akamba started pressuring the government for state-run schools. They also set up their own schools. The government assisted many of the independent schools by supplying and paying the teachers.

Conflict then emerged over who controlled the schools, especially regarding what should be taught. Educated Akamba demanded more academic rather than technical education. These demands increased after the country's first secondary school, Alliance High School, was opened in 1926. Students from Ukambani found it difficult to compete with students from other parts of the country, especially Kikuyuland.

The growth in school attendance was accompanied by expansion in church membership. Christianity made much faster progress than Islam, which was introduced in Ukambani before colonial rule. Akamba Muslims were isolated, and Islam enjoyed none of the support given to the Christian missions.

A number of religious groups also emerged.

Despite the influence of the Christian missions, the Akamba retained many of their traditional beliefs, including their faith in the workings of medicine men.

They often combined ideas from traditional Akamba beliefs, Christianity, and, to a smaller extent, Islam. Examples are the Kitombo (1896), the Kijesu (1906), and Kathambi (1910–11). These groups rejected colonial laws and called for an end to European rule.

The spread of Christianity and Western education affected many aspects of Akamba society and culture. Christianity introduced new

ideas about marriage and family. Polygamy, for example, was strongly opposed.

▼ FORCED LABOR ▼

In addition to political and social changes, Akamba society experienced many economic changes. The colonial government wanted to make the peoples of Central Kenya into laborers for the European farmers who had settled in the region. Some 20 percent of the country's best land was turned over to European settlers. Most of this land was in the highlands of Central Kenya.

The people most affected by this were the livestock-raising Kikuyu and Maasai, but the Akamba also lost some of their most fertile land. In 1908–09 some 4,000 Akamba were expelled from the Mua hills to make room for European ranches. They were not compensated. Through land seizure the government planned to acquire both land and labor for the European farmers. Landless people would have no choice but to look for wage-earning jobs in order to survive.

Taxation was another way to obtain labor. For a person to pay taxes he needed money, which he could earn either by working for wages or selling products. Those Akamba who owned nothing left the Machakos reservation to find work. By 1914 an estimated 1,811 Akamba men worked outside the reserve.

Chiefs and councils of elders in each location were expected to provide a certain number of laborers. Such forced labor was not reliable, however, because workers often ran away. The government and colonial farmers came to depend on the labor of people living or "squatting" on their land.

In the 1920s, the few Akamba farmers who remained expanded their crops to include new ones. But the most profitable crops such as coffee were reserved for European farmers. In the meantime, government control over marketing was tightened. The Akamba were required to sell their produce to government marketing boards, which paid African farmers lower prices than European farmers.

Livestock herds expanded, thanks to improved veterinary services. For a while, the majority of the Akamba got cash by selling livestock and livestock products. Many Akamba opened shops. Their famous wood carving industry developed at this time.

Times became hard for many people in the 1930s. Population had increased, but the amount of available land was limited. As European farms expanded, many squatters were evicted and sent back to the reserve. Finally, land distribution in Ukambani itself was becoming unequal as wealthy farmers bought and controlled more land.

The Akamba reserve became more over-crowded, divided, and tense. Private land ownership spread, and some of the landless became tenants. Others drifted to the town in search of employment. Too much grazing and farming on the same land led to soil erosion. The colonial government tried to persuade the Akamba to sell livestock from severely eroded areas, but the Akamba refused. They pointed out that what was needed was more grazing land.

In 1938 a meat-canning factory opened next to the Akamba reserve on the Athi River. This factory needed 3,000 head of cattle a month to make a profit, but it could not buy more than 1,000. The owners threatened to close the factory and move to Tanganyika. An order was quickly issued authorizing government officials to seize and sell Akamba cattle to the factory. This was known as "destocking."

The destocking order angered the Akamba as never before. The Akamba knew that without livestock they would be forced to enter wage employment in the same numbers as the Kikuyu had been. Through the sale of a cow or some sheep and goats, a family could get enough money to pay taxes and meet its other cash needs. Now they were being asked to part with a quarter or more of their cattle at extremely low prices. Their anger became a nationalistic fervor that helped to end British colonialism.▲

6

AKAMBA NATIONALISM

NATIONALISM IS A WORD USED TO DESCRIBE pride in one's ethnic heritage. It is an awareness that a people or a country has a right to be free, to govern itself, and to preserve its own identity. The destocking campaign lit the fires of Akamba nationalism. The resistance movement was centered in Iveti, the largest, wealthiest, and most populous location in Machakos. Those Akamba who collaborated with the state were cursed and cast out of the community.

In response, the government sent in an armed force and raided 2,500 head of cattle. This only intensified the resistance movement. The Ukamba Members Association (UMA) was formed, modeled on the militant Kikuyu Central Association (KCA), which had begun the fight against colonial rule. The UMA organized a march on Nairobi to meet with the governor.

In the meantime, the antidestocking movement and the UMA had spread to other parts of Ukambani. There were reports of unrest in the Akamba-dominated army and police. An alliance between the UMA and KCA was growing. The government was forced to back down.

Once awakened, Akamba nationalism could not be stopped, even after the destocking order was withdrawn. The Akamba, like other Kenyans, had many complaints besides destocking. In 1940 the government took advantage of the world chaos of World War II to ban the UMA, the KCA, and other political organizations. But the war produced conditions that further fueled African nationalism. Widespread shortages of food and other goods, high inflation, and low prices for African produce provoked strikes in towns and unrest in rural areas.

In the meantime, Eliud Mathu, a Mkamba, was pushing for reforms in the Colonial Legislative Council. Appointed in 1944, Mathu was the first African to sit in the council. He fought for more education, social services, political representation, and labor and land reforms.

Mathu also fought to end the *kipande* registration system. All Africans in Kenya were expected to wear like a dog collar an identity card called *kipande*. If caught without it, they were arrested. The *kipande* was deeply resented, and it was abolished in 1947.

Appointed in 1944, Eliud Mathu was the first African to sit on the Colonial Legislative Council.

In the early 1950s the Mau Mau war for Kenyan independence broke out. The Akamba played an important role in these struggles. One of the leaders who was arrested and tried together with Jomo Kenyatta, the future first president of independent Kenya, was Paul Ngei, a member of the Akamba.▲

7

AKAMBA SOCIETY TODAY

KENYA FINALLY WON INDEPENDENCE IN 1963.
Many of the changes introduced during the
colonial period continued, and some even accel-
erated. Many cultural values and social struc-
tures, including the institutions of marriage and
family, were transformed.

The Akamba of today live quite differently
from the way their grandparents did. They
number over 1.5 million, three quarters of
whom live in the Kamba-dominated districts
of Machakos and Kitui. The rest are scattered
all over Kenya, including the major cities of
Nairobi, Mombasa, Kisumu, and Nakuru.

Most Akamba still live by farming. In addition to the traditional crops, they now grow
coffee, tea, pyrethrum (an insecticide), and
hybrid corn. Since independence, attempts have
been made to dam the rivers, drill water holes,
and construct large-scale irrigation works.

The patterns of agricultural work have changed. With better education, children do less farm work and women are left with more. The participation of men and children in traditional workparties has gradually declined. Wealthier farmers tend to hire wage labor instead of using workparties. If the poor own land, they rely on family labor; otherwise they rent land and become tenants. In short, there is a wider gap between rich and poor in rural areas.

Since independence, however, new self-help groups have emerged in Ukambani and other parts of Kenya. Nationally, this is called the *harambee* movement, often translated as "Let's pull together." In Ukambani, as elsewhere in Kenya, most self-help began with the building of many new schools. Later, attention was focused on projects requiring community action such as building cattle-dips, repairing dams, clearing and extending roads, and collecting money for worthy causes.

Growing numbers of Akamba have left the rural areas for the towns and cities. Some of them need wage employment. Others are educated people who wish to lead an urban life.

More and more, then, Akamba have become dependent on wage employment. Many serve in the police and armed forces. Akamba workers also can be found on farms and in factories

ny Akamba have left the rural areas to search for wage employment in nearby towns and cities.
s man is carving a gazelle, one of thousands of woodcarvings sold to tourists throughout Kenya.

throughout the country and in all the professions.

▼ DECLINE IN TRADITION ▼

The old Akamba political and social institutions have also changed. The councils of elders have lost virtually all their power.

The system of age grades has lost much of its significance. Prestige is based now on education and position in the wider world. The importance of clans has declined as well. While rural Akamba are still able to name their clan, few can name their clan totem.

These changes partly reflect the advances that Christianity and school education have made among the Akamba. As might be expected, older Akamba are more likely to follow the traditional religion than the younger ones. Large-scale conversion to Christianity has affected patterns of marriage and family life. Christians tend to marry in church rather than according to Akamba customs, and they are less likely to practice polygamy.

The Akamba are also less likely to follow traditional initiation rites, especially the women. Young people are marrying earlier; they meet and socialize more easily than before. They can also choose marriage partners more freely. The young generation has new attitudes about the desirable number of children in a family, preferring to have fewer children.

The Akamba have preserved much of their traditional culture despite the difficulties presented by the modern world.

▼ CONCLUSION ▼

Over the past few centuries, the Akamba have experienced many difficult changes. From the start, they adapted to a challenging environment and built complex economic, social, cultural, and political institutions. They became the leading long-distance traders between the Kenyan interior and the coast.

Like many other African peoples at the end of the nineteenth century, the Akamba eventually lost control to British imperialism. However, Akamba society recovered and began adapting to the new situation. The Akamba maintained as much of their independence as possible by expanding their livestock economy. Akamba nationalist struggles, together with others such as the Mau Mau, eventually brought the end of colonialism in Kenya.

Since independence, the Akamba have joined other Kenyans in the difficult task of shaping their country into a new society. They will continue to adapt to the changes of the modern world while at the same time preserving their own culture.▲

Glossary

age grades Important life stages, such as childhood, puberty, marriage, and old age.

bridewealth Cattle or money that a young man must pay to his bride's family.

clan Group of families who trace their history to a common ancestor.

destocking Movement by the British government to force the Kenyan people to sell their livestock.

Harambee (Swahili for "Let's pull together.") Self-help projects that the government encouraged after Kenyan independence.

intercropping Planting more than one kind of crop at the same time in the same field.

irrigation System of ditches to carry water from a river to a very dry part of the land.

Mau Mau A liberation movement in Kenya after World War II.

terracing Method of farming in which big steps are dug in hillsides so that crops can be planted flat instead of on a slope.

transhumance Yearly migration of people from highlands in the summer to plains in the winter, so that there is always grass for cattle grazing.

For Further Reading

Berg-Schlosser, Dirk, *Tradition and Change in Kenya*. Munich: Ferdinand Schoning, 1984.

Hill, Martin J.D. *The Harambee Movement in Kenya*. London: Athlone Press, 1991.

Hobley, C.W. *Bantu Beliefs and Magic*. London: Frank Cass, 1967.

Kavyu, Paul. *Drum Music of Akamba*. Hohenschaftlarn: K. Renner, 1986.

———. *An Introduction to Kamba Music*. Kampala: East African Literature Bureau, 1977.

Kieti, Mwikali. *Barking, You'll Be Eaten: The Wisdom of Kamba Oral Literature*. Nairobi: Phoenix Publ., 1990.

Mbiti, John S. *Akamba Stories*. Oxford: Clarendon Press, 1966.

———. *African Religions and Philosophy*. London: Heinemann, 1980.

———. *English-Kamba Vocabulary*. Nairobi: Eagle Press, 1959.

Nzioko, Sammy. *Akamba*. London: Evans Brothers, 1982.

Index

ABOUT THE AUTHOR
Tiyambe Zeleza was born in Harare, Zimbabwe, and grew up in Malawi. He received a master's degree at the University of London and a Ph.D. in history at Dalhousie University, Halifax, Nova Scotia. He has studied and taught at universities around the world. He is currently an associate professor of history at Trent University, Peterborough, Ontario.

Dr. Zeleza is the author of two works of fiction and several historical works, including *A Modern Economic History of Africa: The Nineteenth Century*. He is coauthor of the four-volume *Themes in Kenyan and World History*.

PHOTO CREDITS: AP/Wide World (pp. 54 and 57), CFM, Nairobi (all other photos)

PHOTO RESEARCH: Vera Ahmadzadeh with Jennifer Croft

DESIGN: Kim Sonsky